Boost Your Reading Skills
CEFR **B1**

BOOK **2**

Success
with
Reading

Maiko Ikeda

Ayaka Shimizu

Zachary Fillingham

Owain Mckimm

Judy Majewski

 **SEIBIDO**

JN035259

音声ファイルのダウンロード／ストリーミング

CD マーク表示がある箇所は、音声を弊社 HP より無料でダウンロード／ストリーミングすることができます。トップページのバナーをクリックし、書籍検索してください。 書籍詳細ページに音声ダウンロードアイコンがございますのでそちらから自習用音声としてご活用ください。

https://www.seibido.co.jp

 ActeaBo

本書はテキスト連動型 Web 教材 ActeaBo に対応しています。ActeaBoでは、各 Unit に 2 編ずつ新たな英文素材が用意されており、授業で学んだリーディング方略や内容理解問題で振り返り学習することができます（本書をご利用期間中の1年間）。ActeaBo のご利用については、先生の指示に従い、ID、パスワードを取得後、下記 URL よりアクセスしてください。

http://acteabo.jp

ID	
パスワード	

※本サービスは教育機関におけるクラス単位でのご利用に限らせていただきます。

Success with Reading Book 2 —Boost Your Reading Skills—

Preface

Success with Reading Book 2 —Boost Your Reading Skills— is the second book of a three-volume series designed mainly to develop reading skills with the aid of learning strategies. High proficiency in English will broaden your horizons and enable you to see a more interesting world.

Each unit of *Success with Reading Book 2* follows a set structure to encourage students to put what they have learned into practice in communication activities. The unit begins with a Tips for Reading section, which introduces a strategy for more effective reading. This is followed by a Vocabulary section in which students check words related to the topic in context. They will then check their comprehension of the passage, both details and main ideas. The unit ends with opportunities for students to express and exchange their ideas regarding the related topics.

As students progress through each level, they are constantly encouraged to put what they have learned to use. At the same time, they never stop taking new challenges that will push them to a new stage. *Success with Reading Book 2* will open up a path to a place where students can look out over a wonderful landscape after enjoying every moment of the journey.

Contents

KEY FOR LEARNING 1
Scanning

KEY FOR LEARNING 2
Paying attention to topic sentences

KEY FOR LEARNING 3
Supporting sentences

LOUIS ARMSTRONG

Learning Overview

KEY FOR LEARNING 1

Scanning

The Pencil

WARM-UP QUESTIONS

Discuss the questions below with your classmates.

1. What do you usually use to write something?
2. How often do you use a pencil?

VOCABULARY

From the choices below, choose the word which fits best in each sentence.

1. We cannot take good health for _____, and so we must try to cultivate a healthy lifestyle.
2. Smartphones are _____ that first appeared in the 2000s.
3. Alexander Graham Bell is very famous as the person who _____ the telephone in 1876.
4. The participants' feedback is used to _____ the course for the next year.
5. We have to _____ a self-addressed envelope with our application forms.
6. The students are graded _____ how much they contribute to the class.
7. The _____ use of smartphones has changed how we arrange to meet people.
8. My mother works at a small factory where bicycles are _____.
9. More and more people are searching for _____ youth.
10. I need your help because I cannot _____ this question by myself.

| according to | devices | enclose | eternal | figure out |
| granted | invented | manufactured | modify | widespread |

10

---

1 WARM-UP QUESTIONS

Introduces warm-up questions to activate the students' background knowledge about the topic.

2 VOCABULARY

Teaches topic-related vocabulary words in a sentence where students can learn the usage of the words.

TIPS FOR READING

Scanning (1)

You may have experienced the feeling of getting lost while reading a passage in English. In this situation, scanning can be useful. Scanning is reading to find the most important information first. You can effectively scan the passage by making use of keywords from the comprehension questions.

Example <u>What</u> is <u>she</u> supposed to do as homework <u>by tomorrow</u>?
         what   who   when

> What, Who, When

EXERCISE

Try to pick up the keywords from the questions below and highlight them. Check them with your partner or teacher.

Questions
a) What are some of the most important technological advances in history?
b) In what situations do you use them now?
c) How long has it been since the first graphite pencil was invented?

11

---

3 TIPS FOR READING

Teaches a reading strategy together with examples and key points.

EXERCISE

Provides an opportunity for using tips for reading introduced above.

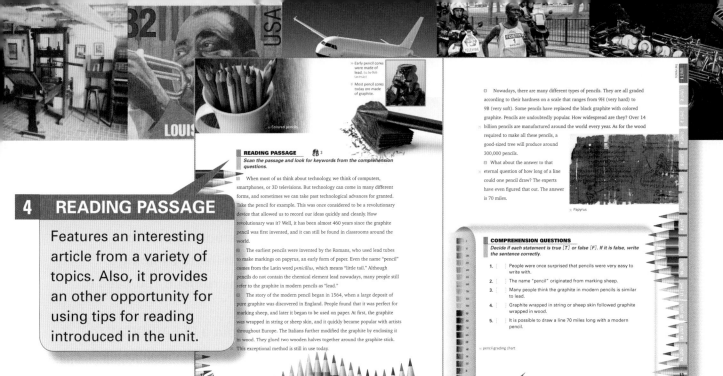

○ Early pencil cores were made of lead. (cc by Rob Levinsky)
○ Most pencil cores today are made of graphite.

○ Colored pencils

4 READING PASSAGE

Features an interesting article from a variety of topics. Also, it provides an other opportunity for using tips for reading introduced in the unit.

READING PASSAGE 🎧 3
Scan the passage and look for keywords from the comprehension questions.

When most of us think about technology, we think of computers, smartphones, or 3D televisions. But technology can come in many different forms, and sometimes we can take past technological advances for granted. Take the pencil for example. This was once considered to be a revolutionary device that allowed us to record our ideas quickly and cleanly. How revolutionary was it? Well, it has been almost 460 years since the graphite pencil was first invented, and it can still be found in classrooms around the world.

The earliest pencils were invented by the Romans, who used lead tubes to make markings on papyrus, an early form of paper. Even the name "pencil" comes from the Latin word *penicillus*, which means "little tail." Although pencils do not contain the chemical element lead nowadays, many people still refer to the graphite in modern pencils as "lead."

The story of the modern pencil began in 1564, when a large deposit of pure graphite was discovered in England. People found that it was perfect for marking sheep, and later it began to be used on paper. At first, the graphite was wrapped in string or sheep skin, and it quickly became popular with artists throughout Europe. The Italians further modified the graphite by enclosing it in wood. They glued two wooden halves together around the graphite stick. This exceptional method is still in use today.

Nowadays, there are many different types of pencils. They are all graded according to their hardness on a scale that ranges from 9H (very hard) to 9B (very soft). Some pencils have replaced the black graphite with colored graphite. Pencils are undoubtedly popular. How widespread are they? Over 14 billion pencils are manufactured around the world every year. As for the wood required to make all these pencils, a good-sized tree will produce around 300,000 pencils.

What about the answer to that eternal question of how long of a line could one pencil draw? The experts have even figured that out. The answer is 70 miles.

○ Papyrus

COMPREHENSION QUESTIONS
Decide if each statement is true [T] or false [F]. If it is false, write the sentence correctly.

1. [ ] People were once surprised that pencils were very easy to write with.
2. [ ] The name "pencil" originated from marking sheep.
3. [ ] Many people think the graphite in modern pencils is similar to lead.
4. [ ] Graphite wrapped in string or sheep skin followed graphite wrapped in wood.
5. [ ] It is possible to draw a line 70 miles long with a modern pencil.

○ pencil grading chart

5 COMPREHENSION QUESTIONS

Introduces comprehension exercises based on the content from Reading passage.

6 GRAPHIC SUMMARY

Introduces a summary-writing exercise which is also useful as an output activity.

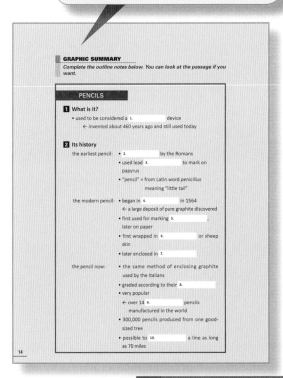

GRAPHIC SUMMARY
Complete the outline notes below. You can look at the passage if you want.

PENCILS

1 What is it?
- used to be considered a 1. _____ device
  ← invented about 460 years ago and still used today

2 Its history
the earliest pencil: • 2. _____ by the Romans
- used lead 3. _____ to mark on papyrus
- "pencil" = from Latin word *penicillus* meaning "little tail"

the modern pencil: • began in 4. _____ in 1564
  ← a large deposit of pure graphite discovered
- first used for marking 5. _____, later on paper
- first wrapped in 6. _____ or sheep skin
- later enclosed in 7. _____

the pencil now: • the same method of enclosing graphite used by the Italians
- graded according to their 8. _____
- very popular
  ← over 14 9. _____ pencils manufactured in the world
- 300,000 pencils produced from one good-sized tree
- possible to 10. _____ a line as long as 70 miles

14

7 WRITING AND DISCUSSION

Introduces questions for output exercise based on the content of the reading passage.

WRITING AND DISCUSSION
Read the questions below and write down your answer below. Exchange your ideas or opinions with your classmates. Use the hints if you want.

1. Apart from pencils, what other products do you think were once revolutionary devices? Why?

   Hints ○ completely changed / our habits / expanded

   Your Ideas

2. What kind of writing tools would you like to have in the future? Why?

   Hints ○ transcribe / sound input / expand

   Your Ideas

8 FURTHER STUDY

Introduces an opportunity for further independent study.

FURTHER STUDY
For further study, access ActeaBo and review today's lesson.

http://acteabo.jp

15

Tips for Reading: Planning for your study

For successful English learning, one of the most important things is to CONTINUE learning it. You cannot master English by studying only for a couple of years. English learning is therefore very similar to climbing mountains, practicing cooking or practicing a music instrument. You need to continue.

However, you cannot continue to learn English without a CLEAR GOAL to achieve. For example, when it comes to climbing a mountain, how high is the mountain? What tools or clothes do you need for climbing? Which route are you going to take? How many days do you need? Without knowing all of this clearly, you cannot maintain your motivation and may soon give up.

Therefore, you need to set a clear goal before restarting your English learning this time. The clearer it is, the more easily you can achieve it. Also, setting SMALLER STEPS to achieve the goal helps you continue learning. Every time you take one step forward, you can feel success and the desire to move forward.

Example

Goal	Reading one passage easily without using a dictionary
Smaller steps	1. Increasing vocabulary (300 more words) 2. Reading faster ← arriving here one year later! 3. Writing a short summary (with a few sentences)

LET'S TRY

Set a clear goal for your English learning. Also, set smaller steps to achieve the goal. Do not forget to indicate where you want to be one year later through learning English with this textbook.

Goal	
Smaller steps	

The Pencil

WARM-UP QUESTIONS

Discuss the questions below with your classmates.

1. What do you usually use to write something?
2. How often do you use a pencil?

VOCABULARY   2

From the choices below, choose the word which fits best in each sentence.

1. We cannot take good health for _____, and so we must try to cultivate a healthy lifestyle.

2. Smartphones are _____ that first appeared in the 2000s.

3. Alexander Graham Bell is very famous as the person who _____ the telephone in 1876.

4. The participants' feedback is used to _____ the course for the next year.

5. We have to _____ a self-addressed envelope with our application forms.

6. The students are graded _____ how much they contribute to the class.

7. The _____ use of smartphones has changed how we arrange to meet people.

8. My mother works at a small factory where bicycles are _____.

9. More and more people are searching for _____ youth.

10. I need your help because I cannot _____ this question by myself.

according to	devices	enclose	eternal	figure out
granted	invented	manufactured	modify	widespread

Scanning (1)

You may have experienced the feeling of getting lost while reading a passage in English. In this situation, scanning can be useful. Scanning is reading to find the most important information first. You can effectively scan the passage by making use of keywords from the comprehension questions.

Example   <u>What</u> is <u>she</u> supposed to do as homework <u>by tomorrow</u>?
    what   who   when

EXERCISE

Try to pick up the keywords from the questions below and highlight them. Check them with your partner or teacher.

Questions

a) What are some of the most important technological advances in history?

b) In what situations do you use them now?

c) How long has it been since the first graphite pencil was invented?

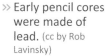

>> Early pencil cores were made of lead. (cc by Rob Lavinsky)

≫ Most pencil cores today are made of graphite.

READING PASSAGE 🔊 3

Scan the passage and look for keywords from the comprehension questions.

1   When most of us think about technology, we think of computers, smartphones, or 3D televisions. But technology can come in many different forms, and sometimes we can take past technological advances for granted. Take the pencil for example. This was once considered to be a revolutionary
5 device that allowed us to record our ideas quickly and cleanly. How revolutionary was it? Well, it has been almost 460 years since the graphite pencil was first invented, and it can still be found in classrooms around the world.

2   The earliest pencils were invented by the Romans, who used lead tubes
10 to make markings on papyrus, an early form of paper. Even the name "pencil" comes from the Latin word *penicillus*, which means "little tail." Although pencils do not contain the chemical element lead nowadays, many people still refer to the graphite in modern pencils as "lead."

3   The story of the modern pencil began in 1564, when a large deposit of
15 pure graphite was discovered in England. People found that it was perfect for marking sheep, and later it began to be used on paper. At first, the graphite was wrapped in string or sheep skin, and it quickly became popular with artists throughout Europe. The Italians further modified the graphite by enclosing it in wood. They glued two wooden halves together around the graphite stick.
20 This exceptional method is still in use today.

THE PENCIL

UNIT 1

UNIT 2

UNIT 3

UNIT 4

UNIT 5

UNIT 6

UNIT 7

UNIT 8

UNIT 9

UNIT 10

UNIT 11

UNIT 12

UNIT 13

UNIT 14

4 Nowadays, there are many different types of pencils. They are all graded according to their hardness on a scale that ranges from 9H (very hard) to 9B (very soft). Some pencils have replaced the black graphite with colored graphite. Pencils are undoubtedly popular. How widespread are they? Over 14 25 billion pencils are manufactured around the world every year. As for the wood required to make all these pencils, a good-sized tree will produce around 300,000 pencils.

5 What about the answer to that 30 eternal question of how long a line could one pencil draw? The experts have even figured that out. The answer is 35 miles.

⌃ Papyrus

COMPREHENSION QUESTIONS

Decide if each statement is true [T] or false [F]. If it is false, write the sentence correctly.

1. [   ] People were once surprised that pencils were very easy to write with.

2. [   ] The name "pencil" originated from marking sheep.

3. [   ] The material lead cannot be found in modern pencils.

4. [   ] Graphite wrapped in string or sheep skin followed graphite wrapped in wood.

5. [   ] It is possible to draw a line 35 miles long with a modern pencil.

F

H

2H

3H

4H

5H

6H

7H

8H

9H

9B

8B

7B

6B

5B

4B

3B

2B

B

HB

« pencil grading chart

13

Complete the outline notes below. You can look at the passage if you want.

PENCILS

1 What is it?
- used to be considered a 1._____ device
  - ← invented about 460 years ago and still used today

2 Its history

the earliest pencil:
- 2._____ by the Romans
- used lead 3._____ to mark on papyrus
- "pencil" = from Latin word *penicillus* meaning "little tail"

the modern pencil:
- began in 4._____ in 1564
  - ← a large deposit of pure graphite discovered
- first used for marking 5._____, later on paper
- first wrapped in 6._____ or sheep skin
- later enclosed in 7._____

the pencil now:
- the same method of enclosing graphite used by the Italians
- graded according to their 8._____
- very popular
  - ← over 14 9._____ pencils manufactured in the world
- 300,000 pencils produced from one good-sized tree
- possible to 10._____ a line as long as 35 miles

UNIT 1
THE PENCIL

UNIT 2
UNIT 3
UNIT 4
UNIT 5
UNIT 6
UNIT 7
UNIT 8
UNIT 9
UNIT 10
UNIT 11
UNIT 12
UNIT 13
UNIT 14

WRITING AND DISCUSSION

Read the questions below and write down your answer below. Exchange your ideas or opinions with your classmates. Use the hints if you want.

1. Apart from pencils, what other products do you think were once revolutionary devices? Why?

   Hints ➲ completely changed / our habits / expanded

   > Your Ideas
   > ....
   > ....
   > ....
   > ....
   > ....

2. What kind of writing tools would you like to have in the future? Why?

   Hints ➲ transcribe / sound input / expand

   > Your Ideas
   > ....
   > ....
   > ....
   > ....
   > ....

FURTHER STUDY

ActeaBo

For further study, access ActeaBo and review today's lesson.

http://acteabo.jp

Scanning

Running Marathons

WARM-UP QUESTIONS

Discuss the questions below with your classmates.

1. What is the longest distance you have run?
2. Who can you name as a famous marathon runner?

VOCABULARY 4

From the choices below, choose the word which fits best in each sentence.

1. The answer is not _____ right, but it is close enough.
2. It is difficult to give a definition of a _____ like "technology."
3. We are _____ with his company for a larger share of the market.
4. The movie festival is held _____ in October.
5. According to _____, the city was destroyed in ancient times by fire from heaven.
6. The _____ from Osaka to Nagoya is shorter than that from Tokyo.
7. When he saw the house, he _____, "What a beautiful house!"
8. Suffering from _____ after the race, he slept for one whole day.
9. Parents are responsible for teaching their children to behave _____ in public.
10. Mike _____ what happened in the family home about 10 years previously.

annually	competing	distance	exactly	exclaimed
exhaustion	legend	properly	recalled	term

Scanning (2)

You may not always find the same keywords in the comprehension questions as in the passage. Another way of scanning is looking for synonyms. A synonym is a word or a phrase that means exactly or nearly the same as another word or phrase.

Example

Comprehension question: How far do you <u>run</u> in a marathon?

synonyms

Sentence: A marathon is a race that <u>covers</u> exactly 42.195 km.

EXERCISE

Find the synonyms from the sample question and the part of the passage below, and highlight them.

Sample question   : Why do many cities hold marathon events today?

Part of the passage : Many big cities now host marathons, which are very popular tourist attractions.

READING PASSAGE 🎵 5

Scan the passage below and look for keywords from the comprehension questions.

1   A marathon is a race that covers exactly 42.195 km. Other long races are sometimes called marathons, but the term is used incorrectly if these races are longer or shorter than 42.195 km.

2   Many big cities now host marathons, which are very popular tourist

5 attractions. Every year, thousands of people travel from all over the world to watch or compete in marathons in London, Berlin, and Boston. Around the world, more than 800 marathons are held annually, with many athletes competing in more than one marathon each year.

3   According to legend, a Greek soldier and messenger by the name of

10 Pheidippides once ran from the town of Marathon to Athens, a distance of about 42 km, without stopping because he carried important news that the Greek army had defeated the Persians at the Battle of Marathon. When he arrived in Athens, Pheidippides exclaimed, "We have won!" Then he dropped to the ground and died from

15 exhaustion.

4   Thankfully, few modern marathon runners die from exhaustion. Today's runners prepare properly and drink enough water while they are competing.

5   In 1896, when the first modern Olympics were held in

20 Athens, officials decided to recall the ancient glory of Greece by hosting a marathon. Since then, the men's marathon has

UNIT 1 | UNIT 2 | UNIT 3 | UNIT 4 | UNIT 5 | UNIT 6 | UNIT 7 | UNIT 8 | UNIT 9 | UNIT 10 | UNIT 11 | UNIT 12 | UNIT 13 | UNIT 14

RUNNING MARATHONS

Samuel Wanjiru in 2007
(cc by Den Haag CPC 2007)

traditionally been the last event of the Games, with the finish line inside the Olympic stadium. In the 2004 Summer Olympics, the traditional route from Marathon to Athens was used for the race, and it ended in Panathinaiko
25 Stadium.

6 At the 2008 Summer Olympics in Beijing, the winner of the men's marathon was Samuel Wanjiru from Kenya, who set an Olympic record with a time of 2:06:32. At the 2012 London Olympics, Ethiopian runner Erba Tiki Galana won the gold medal in the women's marathon, finishing the race with
30 a new Olympic record of 2:23:07.

COMPREHENSION QUESTIONS
Decide if each statement is true [T] or false [F]. If it is false, write the sentence correctly.

1. [   ] The distance of modern marathons is exactly the same as the distance covered by Pheidippides.

2. [   ] Many people have participated in more than one marathon in a year.

3. [   ] Pheidippides failed to tell the news because he was out of breath.

4. [   ] Few marathon runners die today because they are well prepared and drink enough during the race.

5. [   ] At the 2004 Summer Olympics in Athens, the same route was used as the one Pheidippides had run.

GRAPHIC SUMMARY

Complete the outline notes below. You can look at the passage if you want.

RUNNING MARATHONS

1 Actual marathons
- covers **1.** _____ 42.195 km
- no shorter or longer

2 Recent marathons
- popular tourist **2.** _____ in many big cities
  - e.g.) London, Berlin, Boston
- more than 800 marathons annually

3 Its origin
Pheidippides: • a Greek **3.** _____ and messenger
- ran from Marathon to Athens = about 42 km
- was **4.** _____ important news
  - = the Greek army had **5.** _____ the Persians
- ran without **6.** _____
- → died from **7.** _____ (when arriving)

4 In modern Olympics
in 1896   first modern Olympics in Athens

hosted a marathon to **8.** _____ the ancient glory

since then   the men's marathon = the last event of the Games

= **9.** _____ line inside the Olympic stadium

5 Recent records
2008 in Beijing   Samuel Wanjiru from Kenya (the men's marathon)

an Olympic **10.** _____ : 2:06:32

2012 in London   Erba Tiki Galana from Ethiopia (the women's marathon)

new Olympic **10.** _____ : 2:23:07

RUNNING MARATHONS

UNIT 1
UNIT 2
UNIT 3
UNIT 4
UNIT 5
UNIT 6
UNIT 7
UNIT 8
UNIT 9
UNIT 10
UNIT 11
UNIT 12
UNIT 13
UNIT 14

WRITING AND DISCUSSION

Read the questions below and write down your answer below.
Exchange your ideas or opinions with your classmates. Use the hints
if you want.

1. What Olympic events do you like/dislike?

Hints ➡ Sprinting / Gymnastics / Artistic Swimming

> Your Ideas
> ....
> ....
> ....
> ....

2. What sports would you include in Olympics? Why?

Hints ➡ relay / attend / have a chance

> Your Ideas
> ....
> ....
> ....
> ....
> ....

FURTHER STUDY

For further study, access ActeaBo and review today's lesson.

http://acteabo.jp

UNIT 3 — Paying attention to topic sentences

Superstition

WARM-UP QUESTIONS

Discuss the questions below with your classmates.

1. What do you usually do on the day before an important exam?
2. What sort of lucky charms are common in Japan and other countries?

VOCABULARY CD 6

From the choices below, choose the word which fits best in each sentence.

1. An old _____ says that walking under a ladder is unlucky.
2. Her shyness made her say _____ things at the interview.
3. The manager just laughed and _____ my proposal as unrealistic.
4. Last night, I had a _____ dream where I changed into my sister!
5. Her dog enjoyed running around the garden, which was _____ large.
6. I know Chris as I have met him on two separate _____ before.
7. Research has _____ that the risk is higher for men.
8. The company plans to conduct no further _____ with animals.
9. Many shoppers tend to _____ certain brand names with higher quality.
10. For no _____ reason, she quit the part-time job.

| absurd | associate | confirmed | dismissed | experiments |
| fairly | occasions | particular | superstition | weird |

Paying attention to topic sentences (1)

How do you get the key points of a passage? If you read all of the sentences, it will take time. However, in the case of an explanatory passage, you can obtain the important information or ideas more easily by reading the topic sentence of each paragraph.

If you connect all of the topic sentences, you will find it easy to understand the main idea of the passage. The topic sentence is usually the first or the last sentence of each paragraph.

Example

These days, a variety of robots are built to fight one another on television. You may have heard of such robots are Boxbot, Flipper, and Thwackbot. BattleBots is an American company that hosts these robot competitions. It is also the name of a robot-fighting television program. Robot-fighting programs like *BattleBots* and *Robot Wars* have become popular all over the world. Millions of fans watch these programs.

Teams of engineers design and build robots that can cost up to US$50,000 and enter them into those television contests. They give their machines scary or silly names like Vlad the Impaler, The Judge, and Cereal Box Killer. In a BattleBots competition, competitors bring remote-controlled, armored robots armed with weapons and put them into an arena to do their best to destroy each other. There are no limits to how the robots can battle each other.

EXERCISE

Highlight the topic sentences of the second and third paragraphs of the passage on p.24.

UNIT 1
UNIT 2
UNIT 3 SUPERSTITION
UNIT 4
UNIT 5
UNIT 6
UNIT 7
UNIT 8
UNIT 9
UNIT 10
UNIT 11
UNIT 12
UNIT 13
UNIT 14

READING PASSAGE 🎧 7

Read the passage below and use the topic sentences to understand the main idea.

1   Did you know that breaking a mirror will give you seven years of bad luck, or that cutting your nails on a Sunday is just asking for trouble? And do not even think about
5 opening that umbrella indoors; terrible things will happen if you do!

2   Superstitions are powerful, often absurd beliefs that control the way we behave. You may dismiss superstition as
10 something for old ladies or the overly naive, but have you ever worn a pair of lucky socks to an exam or kept a lucky coin in your pocket during a sports game in the hope that it would help you win? Maybe you are more superstitious than you thought. While superstitions themselves may be weird, the reasons why they exist are, in fact, fairly simple.

15 **3**   Think of that time you wore those pink spotted socks to school and happened to do well in a test. It could have been just chance, but the second and third time? Surely that was more than just blind luck. Not necessarily. Human beings often make links between things that are completely unconnected. When, by chance, you wore those socks and
20 got a good test score again, that link became stronger. And what about those times that you wore those ridiculous socks

⌄ Skinner observed pigeons turning
in circles in the hope that food
would appear.

⌃ Blue Turkish eyes, sold as lucky charms
for protection from bad things

and nothing happened? Well, you have probably forgotten those occasions. We tend to selectively remember things that confirm what we want to be true, and forget the things that do not.

25

4 In an experiment by the psychologist B. F. Skinner, pigeons were put in a cage along with a machine that regularly delivered food. The pigeons began associating the delivery of the food with whatever action they had been doing when the food was delivered. Skinner observed pigeons turning in circles, swaying their heads from side to side, or repeatedly going to a particular corner of the cage in the hope that food would appear as a result. They had linked their action with the delivery of food, when in fact the food would come no matter what they did. Sound familiar? Humans may be the smartest of all creatures, but when it comes to superstition, we are just pigeons hoping to be fed.

30

35

40

⌃ B. F. Skinner (1904-1990)
(cc by Silly rabbit)

⌃ Hanging a horseshoe over a door is said to bring good fortune.

COMPREHENSION QUESTIONS

Decide if each statement is true [T] or false [F]. If it is false, write the sentence correctly.

1. [   ] Many old ladies tend to dismiss some absurd superstitions.

2. [   ] Though many superstitions may seem odd, it is easy to understand why we believe them.

3. [   ] When a certain action is repeatedly followed by a good result, we think the two things are probably related.

4. [   ] When nothing happens after wearing dotted pink socks, we are likely to forget this negative result.

5. [   ] The birds in the experiment repeatedly went to a certain corner to choose the food they liked.

UNIT 1
UNIT 2
UNIT 3
SUPERSTITION
UNIT 4
UNIT 5
UNIT 6
UNIT 7
UNIT 8
UNIT 9
UNIT 10
UNIT 11
UNIT 12
UNIT 13
UNIT 14

Complete the outline notes below. You can look at the passage if you want.

SUPERSTITIONS

1 What are they?

= powerful, absurd beliefs that **1.** _____ the way we behave

    e.g.) *negative*   breaking a mirror → 7 years of bad luck

                cutting **2.** _____ on Sunday → ask for trouble

                open umbrella **3.** _____ → terrible things happen

    positive   a pair of socks to school

                → a good exam **4.** _____

                lucky coin in pocket → winning a sports game

    ✳ not for old ladies or the overly **5.** _____

2 Why do they exist?

because we **6.** _____ remember things

           = forget what we do not want to be **7.** _____

3 Experiment by Skinner

8. _____ in a cage :

    - food delivered **9.** _____ by machine

    - begin to **10.** _____ its delivery with any actions they do

→ similar to humans?!

SUPERSTITION

UNIT 1
UNIT 2
UNIT 3
UNIT 4
UNIT 5
UNIT 6
UNIT 7
UNIT 8
UNIT 9
UNIT 10
UNIT 11
UNIT 12
UNIT 13
UNIT 14

WRITING AND DISCUSSION

Read the questions below and write down your answer below.
Exchange your ideas or opinions with your classmates. Use the hints
if you want.

1. What kinds of superstitions have you heard of?

    Hints ➡ figures of / the symbols of / put you in

    > Your Ideas
    >
    > ....
    > ....
    > ....
    > ....

2. Which superstitions do you believe? Why?

    Hints ➡ a four-leaf clover / a tea stalk / a black cat

    > Your Ideas
    >
    > ....
    > ....
    > ....
    > ....

FURTHER STUDY
ActeaBo

For further study, access ActeaBo and review today's lesson.

http://acteabo.jp

The Printing Press

WARM-UP QUESTIONS

Discuss the questions below with your classmates.

1. What can you find around you that was printed by a printing press?
2. What was happening in Japan around 1450?

VOCABULARY   CD 8

From the choices below, choose the word which fits best in each sentence.

1. Rome is famous for its _____ monuments such as the Colosseum.
2. Smaller vehicles usually _____ less fuel.
3. Fortunately, the flu affected only a tiny _____ of the population.
4. The young couple _____ their initials into a tree.
5. He has been _____ a collection of his favorite books.
6. Plastic door frames are more _____ than wood.
7. These batteries are old and need to be _____ .
8. The concert was an _____ success: the players received a standing ovation.
9. I have just recalled that I still _____ him for the concert tickets.
10. A rash business decision left her $ 600 in _____.

ancient	assembling	astounding	carved	consume
debt	durable	fraction	owe	replaced

Pay attention to topic sentences (2)

You may not always understand the topic sentences perfectly. When that happens, pick up a few keywords from each topic sentence. By connecting all of the keywords together, you can still get the gist of the passage.

Example

word you do not understand   **keywords**

1 Albatrosses are the largest flying birds in the world ....

....

2 An albatross's diet consists of squid, fish, and other small sea

animals. ....

3 Some scientists believe that albatross couples perform special

dances together in order to make their relationship last longer. ....

....

4 When they fly, albatrosses use their long wings to glide through

air that is rising. ....

5 Albatrosses are currently threatened with extinction because of

several factors. ....

EXERCISE

Read the first two paragraphs of the passage on p. 30. From their topic sentences, pick up a few keywords and try to understand the beginning of the story.

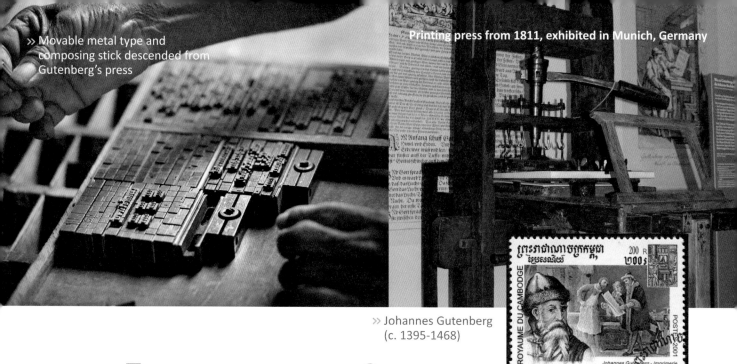

>> Movable metal type and composing stick descended from Gutenberg's press

Printing press from 1811, exhibited in Munich, Germany

>> Johannes Gutenberg (c. 1395-1468)

READING PASSAGE   9

Read the passage below and use topic sentences to understand the main idea.

1   What do you think is mankind's most important invention? Is it the computer, the telephone, or the wheel? Many people say that it is the printing press, a machine that allows us to reproduce unlimited copies of books and documents.

5 **2**   Before the printing press, books were copied by hand. Ancient Roman book publishers sometimes sold as many as 5,000 copies of a book that had been copied by slaves. But copying a book was such a time-consuming and expensive activity that often only a few copies of each book were made. As a result, only a small fraction of the population had

10 access to books and learned to read.

3   While the printing press was invented in 1450 by Johannes Gutenberg, a goldsmith from Germany, printing had already been around for quite some time. Around 5,000 years ago in ancient Mesopotamia, carved stones serving as seals or stamps were used

15 to make impressions in clay. Later in China, wooden blocks were used to carve text, coated in ink and then pressed onto paper or cloth. Instead of using a page-sized block of carved wood, however, Gutenberg's printing press used small, metal blocks,

>> "Modern Book Printing" sculpture in Germany commemorating inventor Gutenberg
(cc by Lienhard Schulz)

UNIT 1
UNIT 2
UNIT 3
THE PRINTING PRESS   UNIT 4
UNIT 5
UNIT 6
UNIT 7
UNIT 8
UNIT 9
UNIT 10
UNIT 11
UNIT 12
UNIT 13
UNIT 14

20 each with just a single letter. To print a page, all the printer had to do was assemble the necessary letters and start the machine. Whereas wooden blocks would quickly become damaged, the metal letter blocks were durable, and if one was found to have a flaw, it could easily be replaced without affecting the entire page. What Gutenberg achieved with his printing press was the ability to mass-produce books quickly, cheaply, and efficiently.

25 ❹   After 1450, thousands of copies of a popular book or newspaper could be printed rapidly and inexpensively. Books and newspapers with ideas and images from all over the world became widely available to the public. The impact of Gutenberg's machine is sometimes compared to the impact of the Internet, as it has allowed millions

30 of people to gain access to new and exciting knowledge. As knowledge fuels human intelligence, mankind's astounding technological and scientific progress over the last 500 years

35 owes no small debt to Gutenberg's remarkable printing press.

⌃ Gutenberg press replica at the Featherbed Alley Printshop Museum in Bermuda
(cc by Aodhdubh)

COMPREHENSION QUESTIONS

Decide if each statement is true [T] or false [F]. If it is false, write the sentence correctly.

1. [   ] It took a huge amount of time and money to make copies of books in ancient Rome.

2. [   ] Johannes Gutenberg invented printing in 1450.

3. [   ] In China, people used wooden blocks to print designs on their clothes.

4. [   ] Before 1450, people needed to print the whole page again if a flaw was found.

5. [   ] Gutenberg's invention is sometimes considered to be greater than the Internet.

any of Ideas
•••••

Complete the outline notes below. You can look at the passage if you want.

THE PRINTING PRESS

1 What is it?

- a machine to reproduce 1. [_____] copies of books or documents
- most important innovation in our lives

2 Before its invention

- copied by 2. [_____]

  e.g.) publishers made 3. [_____] copy the original 5,000 times

  → only a limited number of people had 4. [_____] to books and learned to 5. [_____]

- around 5,000 years ago in Mesopotamia

  carved 6. [_____] to mark in clay

- later in China

  7. [_____] blocks pressed onto paper (page-sized)

- 1450 in Germany

  small metal blocks with a single 8. [_____] each

3 After its birth

- ability to 9. [_____] books quickly, cheaply, and efficiently
  → books and newspapers widely available to 10. [_____]
  → access to new and exciting knowledge for millions of people

WRITING AND DISCUSSION

Read the questions below and write down your answer below.
Exchange your ideas or opinions with your classmates. Use the hints
if you want.

1. How do you think the world changed after books and other documents were mass-produced?

   Hints ➲ advertisement / education / standard

Your Ideas
....
....
....
....
....

2. Do you prefer reading on paper or on screens? Why?

   Hints ➲ overall pages / huge amounts of documents / search

Your Ideas
....
....
....
....
....

FURTHER STUDY

For further study, access ActeaBo and review today's lesson.

http://acteabo.jp

UNIT 1
UNIT 2
UNIT 3
UNIT 4
THE PRINTING PRESS
UNIT 5
UNIT 6
UNIT 7
UNIT 8
UNIT 9
UNIT 10
UNIT 11
UNIT 12
UNIT 13
UNIT 14

How Safe Is Air Travel?

WARM-UP QUESTIONS

Discuss the questions below with your classmates.

1. Which form of transportation do you prefer, car or plane? Why?

2. Why do you think people are afraid of traveling by air?

VOCABULARY 🎧 10

From the choices below, choose the word which fits best in each sentence.

1. How can we _____ spending so much money on weapons?

2. A recent ___ _____ found that the approval rate for the government is below 30%.

3. Government _____ published today indicate that unemployment is dropping.

4. The size of the class was _____ cut to allow for small-group instruction.

5. The biggest quake yesterday _____ 5.0 on the Richter scale.

6. The school bus was involved in a _____ with a car.

7. Electronic payment _____ the need for cash or checks.

8. He has been absent from class _____ illness.

9. The store _____ the cost of repairs at ¥5,000.

10. Her back injury may _____ her from playing in tomorrow's game.

collision	drastically	due to	eliminates	estimated
figures	justify	prevent	registered	survey

Supporting sentences (1)

Once you have got the gist from the topic sentence, you may still be anxious about not understanding the rest of the passage. It will mostly contain supporting sentences such as examples, descriptions, definitions, etc. In supporting sentences, the author gives detailed information to help convey his/her message to the reader.

Example

Scotland makes up the northern third of Great Britain and has
— topic sentence
some of the most incredible scenery in all of the United Kingdom.

If you visit Scotland's west coast, the view might seem oddly familiar to you. Why? The route taken by the Hogwarts Express in the Harry Potter movies is an actual train route in western Scotland.
— supporting sentences (examples)

EXERCISE

Check the main idea of the first paragraph on p. 36 by reading the topic sentence. Then, search for what is written in the supporting sentences.

Main idea	
Supporting idea(s)	

Pilot

Airplane

READING PASSAGE 🎧 11

Read the passage below and pay attention to the relationship between topic sentences and supporting sentences of each paragraph.

1   Have you ever been in an airplane during rough weather? There are few things more frightening than being thousands of feet in the air and unsure of whether you will come down safely again. But is that fear really justified?

2   A survey done in the United States in 2001 found that 20% of Americans were afraid of flying. Of these, one in six people got scared just stepping onto an airplane. Unfortunately, the events of September 11, 2001, made those figures rise even higher, with people increasingly afraid of terrorist attacks as well as things like engine failure or lightning strikes. Fear of flying may have increased after 9/11, but airports and airlines everywhere have stepped up their security efforts, making the likelihood of an attack extremely low.

3   Better training of air traffic controllers and pilots has also drastically decreased the number of crashes that have occurred over the last decade or so. For example, according to the Aircraft Crashes Record Office, in 2012 there were 119 registered crashes. This was down from 194 in 2002 and 262 in 1992. Many kinds of accidents, like mid-air collisions, have been almost totally eliminated due to technical advances in in-flight controls and autopilot systems.

4   Here is something else to consider: you are more

likely to be killed driving to or from the airport than on the flight itself.
The National Transportation Safety Board (NTSB) in the United States

25 estimates that the chance of being killed in a car accident in the United
States is about one in 5,000. However, the chance of being in an aircraft
accident is one in 2,000,000, and there is even a 60% chance that you will
survive that crash.

5   Part of the fear of flying, it seems, is the fear of the unknown. People

30 do not understand exactly how an airplane flies or what systems are in
place to prevent crashes, and this can make people feel uneasy and afraid.
They may also be unaware that
modern airplanes are strong and the
pilots are incredibly well trained. So

35 now that you know how safe flying is,
you can relax the next time you fly.

>> The chances of dying in a car crash
are higher than the chances of
dying in an airplane crash.

COMPREHENSION QUESTIONS

*Decide if each statement is true [T] or false [F]. If it is false,
write the sentence correctly.*

1. [　] One in five people in the US said they were scared of
flying.

2. [　] About 20% of Americans were very anxious about
stepping on an airplane.

3. [　] There were fewer crashes in 2002 than 10 years before.

4. [　] Many accidents in the past happened as a result of
automatic flight systems.

5. [　] Being in a car accident is 400 times more likely than
being in a plane accident.

Complete the outline notes below. You can look at the passage if you want.

HOW SAFE IS AIR TRAVEL?

1 Fear of flying?

• has increased since the 9/11 attack

BUT

• increased safety by:

a) stepping up ___1.___

b) better training of ___2.___ ___3.___

___4.___

• more chances to be killed: in ___5.___ > ___6.___

2 Reason for fear

= fear of ___7.___

← not understand:

- how an airplane ___8.___

- what systems are in place to ___9.___ crashes

- how strong airplanes are

- how well the pilots are ___10.___

UNIT 1
UNIT 2
UNIT 3
UNIT 4
UNIT 5
UNIT 6
UNIT 7
UNIT 8
UNIT 9
UNIT 10
UNIT 11
UNIT 12
UNIT 13
UNIT 14

HOW SAFE IS AIR TRAVEL?

WRITING AND DISCUSSION

Read the questions below and write down your answer below.
Exchange your ideas or opinions with your classmates. Use the hints
if you want.

1. Is there anything you are very afraid of? What is it? Why?

> *Hints* ➡ heights / closed places / darkness

> **Your Ideas**
> ....
> ....
> ....
> ....
> ....

2. What forms of transportation do you prefer for traveling? Why?

> *Hints* ➡ buses / trains / planes

> **Your Ideas**
> ....
> ....
> ....
> ....
> ....

FURTHER STUDY

For further study, access ActeaBo and review today's lesson.

http://acteabo.jp

Supporting sentences

Jazz Music

WARM-UP QUESTIONS

Discuss the questions below with your classmates.

1. What kind of music do you like? Why?
2. What do you think of jazz music?

VOCABULARY   🎵 12

From the choices below, choose the word which fits best in each sentence.

1. When I arrived home, the house was a complete _____.
2. She tackled her new challenging job with _____ and determination.
3. My niece has been indoors all day, and is getting _____.
4. When I started playing, another player started _____ around me.
5. The designers made _____ costumes for last year's Halloween party.
6. Hundreds of mourners attended the _____ of the singer.
7. Hundreds of people marched in _____ to the Capitol building.
8. I like Italian _____, particularly Puccini.
9. His performance elicited _____ applause and a standing ovation.
10. The government announced tougher _____ on tobacco advertising.

composers	elaborate	funeral	improvising	mess
procession	restless	restrictions	spontaneous	vigor

Supporting sentences (2)

Once you understand the relationship between a topic sentence and its supporting sentences, you can make a good summary. It may look like a map with landmarks (topic sentences) and details (supporting sentences).

Example

> Scotland: - north + 1/3 of UK
>
> - incredible scenery
>
> e.g.) west coast = Harry Potter movies!

EXERCISE

Make notes for a summary of Paragraph 1 of the passage on p. 42. First, pick up a few keywords from the topic sentences. Then, add some more keywords from the supporting sentences.

> **Summary of Paragraph 1**

>> Louis Armstrong was a much-imitated innovator of early jazz.

JAZZ COMPOSER AND TRUMPETER

32

USA

LOUIS ARMSTRONG

READING PASSAGE 13

Read the passage below and pay attention to supporting sentences.

1   To some, jazz sounds like a musical mess; to others it is the most
expressive and animated form of music around, a combination of styles and
musical traditions that reflects the blended nature of the culture in which it
developed.

2   Jazz originated in the early 20th century in the United States, particularly
in the cities of New Orleans and Chicago. The word "jazz" is thought to
have begun as a West Coast slang word meaning "spirit" or "vigor." The first
recorded usage of the word appears far away from the New Orleans music
scene, in the sports pages of a West Coast newspaper in 1912, where it was
used to describe the unpredictable curve of a certain baseball player's pitch.
Around 1915, however, "jazz" was first used to refer to the kind of restless,
improvised music emerging in Chicago at the time.

3   A combination of spiritual music, blues, ragtime, and even military music,
jazz owes a large part of its development to the elaborate funeral processions
held by African-American communities of New Orleans. Many of the early
jazz musicians played at these processions, and as a result, the instruments of
the marching band—like drums, trumpets, and trombones—became the basic
instruments of jazz.

4 Though jazz's early influences are clear, jazz itself is very difficult to define.

20 This is because one of the most important parts of jazz is improvisation. In jazz, a performer may change melodies, harmonies, or time signatures at will. Whereas European classical music is sometimes seen as a composer's music, with the performer's role being mainly to play the music as the composer intended, jazz is often seen as being under the control of the musicians

25 themselves. A jazz song is spontaneous; it develops naturally from the performers' interactions with each other on stage. It is not planned or under the restrictions of strict rules. This has allowed jazz to produce countless subgenres: bebop, swing, cool jazz, acid jazz, free jazz, jazz-funk and jazz rap being only a few examples.

COMPREHENSION QUESTIONS

Decide if each statement is true [T] or false [F]. If it is false, write the sentence correctly.

1. [   ] Jazz can be compared to American society in terms of its mixture of different kinds of music or people.

2. [   ] The word "jazz" first referred to a kind of baseball pitch.

3. [   ] Jazz music influenced the style of marching in funerals in the US.

4. [   ] In the original style of jazz, the musicians needed to play what the composer wrote on the score.

5. [   ] The spontaneous nature of jazz has led to the birth of subgenres.

Complete the outline notes below. You can look at the passage if you want.

JAZZ MUSIC

1 Its history

- 1. [_____] in early 20th century
- "jazz" = " 2. [_____]" or "vigor"
- 1912 appeared first in the 3. [_____] pages of the newspaper
- 1915 restless, improvised music in Chicago
- developed from 4. [_____] 5. [_____] by African-American communities

    instruments of the 6. [_____] 7. [_____]
    e.g.) drums, trumpets, trombones

2 Its characteristics

- improvisation = change melodies, harmonies, or time signatures
    at performer's 8. [_____]
- spontaneous = develop from the performers' 9. [_____]
    = led to many subgenres
- ⟷ Western classical music = 10. [_____]'s music

UNIT 1
UNIT 2
UNIT 3
UNIT 4
UNIT 5
JAZZ MUSIC   UNIT 6
UNIT 7
UNIT 8
UNIT 9
UNIT 10
UNIT 11
UNIT 12
UNIT 13
UNIT 14

WRITING AND DISCUSSION

Read the questions below and write down your answer below.
Exchange your ideas or opinions with your classmates. Use the hints
if you want.

1. Why do you think African-American communities in New Orleans held elaborate funeral processions?

   Hints ➲ express / sorrow / encourage

   > Your Ideas
   >
   > ....
   > ....
   > ....
   > ....
   > ....

2. When do you think Japanese pop music started? How has it developed since then?

   Hints ➲ mass media / lyrics / Japanese traditional ballad

   > Your Ideas
   >
   > ....
   > ....
   > ....
   > ....
   > ....

FURTHER STUDY

For further study, access ActeaBo and review today's lesson.

http://acteabo.jp

UNIT **7**

Inflation

WARM-UP QUESTIONS

Discuss the questions below with your classmates.

1. How much money do you make per hour at your part-time job?

2. How much do you think the hourly wage was 10 years ago? How much will it be in 10 years?

VOCABULARY   🎧 14

From the choices below, choose the word which fits best in each sentence.

1. I have recently started growing vegetables in my _____.

2. Through online communication, people can _____ contact with each other.

3. A half day's activities will _____ us £30.

4. The company's success led to an _____ in the number of stores it opened last year.

5. Many fine wines increase in _____ as they get older.

6. Lack of sleep can be a _____ for a wide range of diseases.

7. Good training will give a beginner the _____ to enjoy skating.

8. The government broadened its _____ of "small business" to help support young entrepreneurs.

9. A limited number of £12 tickets are _____ from the box office.

10. My aunt has a _____ cough because of her smoking.

| available | backyard | confidence | cost | definition |
| expansion | maintain | persistent | trigger | value |

Paying attention to discourse markers (1)

Discourse markers help us better understand the structure of a passage.
Reading without these words is like walking in the forest without any signs.
Below are some examples of useful discourse markers.

Example

Contrastive	but, however, nevertheless
Inferential	therefore, then
Ordering	first, next, then, second, finally
Cause / Effect	because, due to

EXERCISE

Highlight the discourse markers in Paragraphs 1 and 2 of the passage on
p. 48. Try using them to understand the structure of the passage.

	Discourse markers	Structure of the paragraph
Paragraph 1		
Paragraph 2		

READING PASSAGE 15

Read the passage below and pay attention to discourse markers.

⌄ Inflation is when the cost of goods and services rises.

1   Jim took the $10 he had been saving carefully for months and buried it in his backyard. Forty years passed before he finally decided to dig it up and buy something nice.
5 The only problem was that by 2012, his $10 was not even enough to buy an iPhone case for his grandson.

2   What happened? Although Jim's money maintained its original face value, it was not worth as much because
10 everything had become more expensive. Jim forgot about inflation.

3   Inflation is when the cost of goods and services rises in an economy. It is generally seen as a negative economic force because rising prices can eat away at a household's finances. Governments and central banks try their best to control inflation, and they do so by trying to keep the inflation rate under
15 three percent.

4   There are several economic factors that can cause inflation. The first is the expansion of a country's money supply. If there is more money being printed, the money's purchasing power goes down, and prices will go up as a result. Inflation can also be caused by demand for a product
20 exceeding the amount of available supply. Another trigger for inflation is an increase in the price of items or materials needed to produce a good or service. For example, because gasoline is needed to power tractors on farms, an increase in the price of gas will cause food prices to go up as well.

5 Inflation can sometimes spin out of control when a population loses

Gas

Sky Hi

Expensi

Modera

Reasonabl

Cheap

UNIT 1
UNIT 2
UNIT 3
UNIT 4
UNIT 5
UNIT 6
INFLATION
UNIT 7
UNIT 8
UNIT 9
UNIT 10
UNIT 11
UNIT 12
UNIT 13
UNIT 14

« When inflation occurs, the value of money decreases.

all confidence in the value of its money. This is called "hyperinflation."
While there are several different definitions, most economists agree that
30 hyperinflation occurs when a country's monthly inflation rate exceeds 50
percent. At a rate that high, money is losing half of its value every month.

6   There are many historical examples of hyperinflation wreaking havoc
on a country's economy. In China in 1947, the highest yuan bill available
was 50,000. By 1949, the government was issuing 500,000,000-yuan bills.
35 Similar inflation crises took place in Germany during the 1920s, France during
the French Revolution, and Argentina during the 1980s. The government of
Zimbabwe has also been fighting a persistent hyperinflation crisis since 2008.

COMPREHENSION QUESTIONS

Decide if each statement is true [T] or false [F]. If it is false, write the sentence correctly.

1. [   ] Jim buried a $10 bill to be able to spend it at a later time.

2. [   ] Inflation is said to raise the value of a household's savings.

3. [   ] Hyperinflation occurs when people do not believe their money has any value.

4. [   ] In hyperinflation, a ¥10,000 bill will have a value of ¥15,000 in the next month.

5. [   ] In China, the value of money decreased about 10,000 times in the two years after 1947.

Complete the outline notes below. You can look at the passage if you want.

INFLATION

1 Episode

$10 buried

↓ 40 years

2012 not even enough to buy an iPhone case

2 What is it?

- when **1.** _____ rise in an economy
- can affect a **2.** _____ finances
- governments and **3.** _____ banks try to control
  by keeping the **4.** _____ under 3%

3 Its cause

a) expansion of money **5.** _____

b) demand **6.** _____ supply

c) increase in price of **7.** _____ needed to produce a good
   or service

4 Hyperinflation

- inflation rate **8.** _____ 50%
  = money loses half of its **9.** _____ every month
    e.g.) during the French **10.** _____
            1920s in Germany
            1947 in China
            1980s in Argentina
            2008 in Zimbabwe

WRITING AND DISCUSSION

Read the questions below and write down your answer below. Exchange your ideas or opinions with your classmates. Use the hints if you want.

1. Name some products whose demand exceeds its available supply.

      Hints ➡ gasoline / hotel room / Olympic tickets

> **Your Ideas**
>
> ....
>
> ....
>
> ....
>
> ....
>
> ....

2. How much was your favorite food several years ago? Why do you think its price has risen or dropped?

      Hints ➡ cost / result from / due to

> **Your Ideas**
>
> ....
>
> ....
>
> ....
>
> ....
>
> ....

FURTHER STUDY

For further study, access ActeaBo and review today's lesson.

http://acteabo.jp

The Word "Hello"

WARM-UP QUESTIONS

Discuss the questions below with your classmates.

1. Are you good at talking to someone you do not know? Why?

2. What do you say when you first meet someone?

VOCABULARY 🔵 16

From the choices below, choose the word which fits best in each sentence.

1. The shop owner demonstrated the _____ of the watch to the customer.

2. I have no _____ toward our teacher, but my classmates dislike her.

3. She _____ the flour with the butter and salt to make pancakes.

4. There is a lot of information that Meg is not releasing, and she is _____ to answer questions.

5. His work _____ described him as a person who puts a smile on everyone's face.

6. He _____ his wonderful sense of humor and makes everyone laugh.

7. I like this town because everyone is _____ to me all the time.

8. The manager is able to identify problems instantly and act _____.

9. My mother can recognize _____ variations of tastes when she cooks.

10. A simple difference of _____ explained their different results.

accordingly	colleagues	combined	friendly	hostility
interpretation	mechanism	refusing	retains	slight

Paying attention to discourse markers (2)

When you read with a focus on conjunctions and conjunctive adverbs, you can more easily understand the storyline of a passage. Then, you can take good notes by using symbols and abbreviations. Here is an example of notes from Paragraph 3 in Unit 7.

Example

Inflation   :   — the rising cost of goods

+ services in economy

— seen as negative

← eat away at household finances

↓

Governments :   try to keep inflation rate under 3%

+ central banks

EXERCISE

Take notes for Paragraph 1 of the passage on p. 54, paying attention to discourse markers. Then, compare your notes with your classmates.

UNIT 1
UNIT 2
UNIT 3
UNIT 4
UNIT 5
UNIT 6
UNIT 7
UNIT 8 *THE WORD "HELLO"*
UNIT 9
UNIT 10
UNIT 11
UNIT 12
UNIT 13
UNIT 14

Read the passage below and pay attention to discourse markers.

1 "Hello" is a powerful word with immeasurable spiritual value because it provides you with a mechanism to start new relationships and develop existing
5 ones. Your failure to offer a simple greeting can result in a cold shoulder or even open hostility. "Hello" functions as a social lubricant similar to other polite expressions such as "thank you" or "good afternoon." These types of polite expressions are essential for building relationships between people.

10 **2** Merely saying the word "hello" can pave the way to a friendly exchange of comments about the weather or news. If you combine the word "hello" with a hearty smile, you will be regarded as amiable, outgoing, and trustworthy. In contrast, if you refuse to use such niceties, you may be viewed as depressed, rude, aloof, or unfriendly. So, if you want to have a nice day at work or
15 at school, say "Hello," and flash a big smile when you see your colleagues and boss or your classmates and teachers.

3 In various corners of the English-speaking world, local flavors of the word "hello" have led to a colorful range of greetings. No matter which form it takes, the word retains its essentially
20 friendly meaning. So, when you hear "Hi," "How do you do," "Hiya," "Wazzup," "Howdy," or "Hey," you know that someone is saying "Hello," and you should respond accordingly.

>> "Hello" is a powerful word.

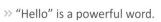

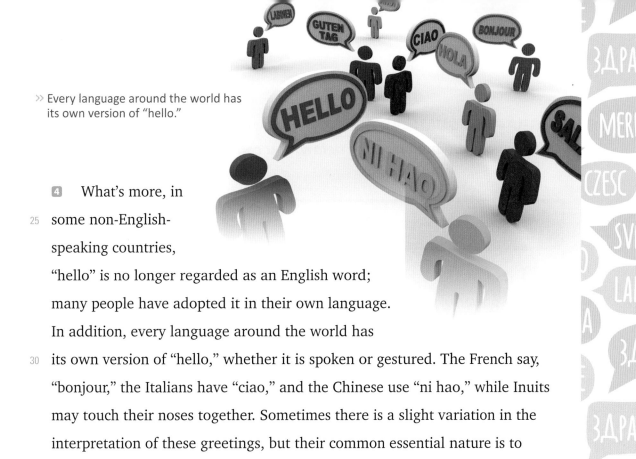

UNIT 1
UNIT 2
UNIT 3
UNIT 4
UNIT 5
UNIT 6
UNIT 7
UNIT 8
THE WORD "HELLO"
UNIT 9
UNIT 10
UNIT 11
UNIT 12
UNIT 13
UNIT 14

>> Every language around the world has its own version of "hello."

④   What's more, in

25   some non-English-

speaking countries,

"hello" is no longer regarded as an English word; many people have adopted it in their own language. In addition, every language around the world has

30   its own version of "hello," whether it is spoken or gestured. The French say, "bonjour," the Italians have "ciao," and the Chinese use "ni hao," while Inuits may touch their noses together. Sometimes there is a slight variation in the interpretation of these greetings, but their common essential nature is to create goodwill and trust.

35   ⑤   "Hello" might strike you as a simple, irrelevant word, but you should never underestimate its importance.

COMPREHENSION QUESTIONS

Decide if each statement is true [T] or false [F]. If it is false, write the sentence correctly.

1. [   ] The word "hello" is a powerful word that is easy to use.

2. [   ] Failure to offer a simple greeting can cause a cold shoulder or even an unfriendly situation.

3. [   ] If you say "hello" with a big smile, you can have a nice day at work or at school.

4. [   ] When you hear local versions of the word "hello," you should not respond to it.

5. [   ] The Inuit version of "hello" may involve touching noses.

Complete the outline notes below. You can look at the passage if you want.

THE WORD "HELLO"

1 Its functions
- powerful word to start new relationship + develop
  1. _____ ones
- functions as a **2.** _____ lubricant
  e.g.) "thank you" "good afternoon"
- essential for **3.** _____ relationship between people
- encourage a friendly exchange of comments
  e.g.) hello with a **4.** _____ smile → **5.** _____ ,
  outgoing, and trustworthy
  ↔ refuse → **6.** _____ , rude, aloof, or unfriendly

2 in English-speaking world
- colorful range of greetings
BUT
- retain its essentially friendly meaning → should **7.** _____
  accordingly

3 in non-English speaking countries
- **8.** _____ in their own language
- have their own version of "hello"
- a slight variation in the **9.** _____
BUT
essentially to create **10.** _____ and trust

WRITING AND DISCUSSION

Read the questions below and write down your answer below.
Exchange your ideas or opinions with your classmates. Use the hints
if you want.

1. What do you think of not greeting someone when you first meet?

   Hints ➲ rude / do not care / further conversation

Your Ideas
....
....
....
....

2. Instead of saying "hello," how else can we start a conversation?

   Hints ➲ bow / shake hands / smile

Your Ideas
....
....
....
....

FURTHER STUDY

For further study, access ActeaBo and review today's lesson.

http://acteabo.jp

Trans Fats

WARM-UP QUESTIONS

Discuss the questions below with your classmates.

1. What do you usually have for lunch?
2. What kinds of food do you think contain trans fats?

VOCABULARY 🔊 18

From the choices below, choose the word which fits best in each sentence.

1. A friend suggested I could burn more _____ by doing strength training.
2. The veterinarian prevented my pet from getting a more _____ disease.
3. Mix together all the other _____ with a spoon.
4. She accidentally _____ her mother's old diary in the closet.
5. The girl _____ played her favorite song when she became sad.
6. If Mike has not fully recovered, his likely _____ will be Suzanne.
7. Students used to know how to _____ attention to boring lectures.
8. After one deep breath, she stepped into the _____ to perform.
9. You have to be careful to take medicine which _____ your blood pressure.
10. My classmate _____ that I read this recently published book.

deadly	discovered	fat	frequently	ingredients
lowers	pay	recommended	spotlight	substitute

Time order (1)

When you read a biography or an explanatory text, the time order is important. Time words can be useful for understanding the order of events. Here are some examples of such words:

Example

Year	in the 2000s, since 1998
Term	for ten years, during the night

EXERCISE

Paying attention to the time words, read Paragraph 3 of the passage on p. 60. Compare your notes with your classmates.

Time words	Notes

Trans fats are a popular ingredient in processed foods like fast food.

⌃ Milk and meat from cows contains naturally occurring trans fats in small quantities.

READING PASSAGE 🎧 19

Read the passage below and pay attention to time words.

1 The story of trans fat is an interesting one because it involves a discovery that started out as a miracle and ended up being deadly.

2 Trans fats are the result of an industrial process that thickens vegetable oils in order to make them more solid. They are also called "partially
5 hydrogenated oils." Trans fats occur naturally in small amounts in many kinds of meat. However, they are also a popular ingredient in many processed foods, like canned soup, packaged snacks, and frozen dinners.

3 The process of hydrogenating oils was first discovered in the 1890s by Paul Sabatier. The discovery enabled the production of margarine, which is
10 still frequently used as a substitute for butter. An early trans-fat product was Crisco, which first went on sale in 1920. Crisco was a lard replacement that was used in baking bread, pies, cookies, and cakes. Up until the 1950s, trans fats were seen as a wonderful invention because they were cheaper
15 than animal-based alternatives and most people agreed that they tasted better. The situation began to change in the 1960s.

4 From 1960 onward, scientific studies began to be published indicating that trans fats
20 were bad for our health. At first, no one paid much attention to them, especially not the food

⌃ Paul Sabatier (1854-1941)

UNIT 1
UNIT 2
UNIT 3
UNIT 4
UNIT 5
UNIT 6
UNIT 7
UNIT 8
UNIT 9
UNIT 10
UNIT 11
UNIT 12
UNIT 13
UNIT 14

TRANS FATS

corporations that were making lots of money from the sale of trans-fat products. It was not until the 1990s that the spotlight really fell on the health

25 risks associated with trans fats. Studies found that trans fats increase bad cholesterol levels while lowering good cholesterol, leading to an increased risk of heart disease, stroke, and diabetes. Most studies concluded that trans fats greatly contribute

30 to the high rate of Americans who die each year from heart disease—more than 500,000.

5 Given the risk, it is probably a good idea to keep an eye out for trans fats in your favorite foods. The American Heart Association

35 recommends limiting your trans-fat intake to 1% of your daily calories. Luckily, most countries have now passed laws requiring food companies to clearly label the amount of trans fat in their products.

What Every Restaurant and Food Service Establishment Needs to Know About Trans Fat

NYC health

≫ Poster from New York City's Board of Health encouraging consumers to limit trans-fat consumption

COMPREHENSION QUESTIONS

Decide if each statement is true [T] or false [F]. If it is false, write the sentence correctly.

1. [ ] Hydrogenated oils are a popular ingredient in many processed foods.

2. [ ] Trans fats have been seen as a wonderful invention since the 1950s.

3. [ ] Trans fats were welcomed at first by people because they added flavor.

4. [ ] No one initially paid attention to the research on trans fats, especially food corporations.

5. [ ] Few countries have passed laws requiring food companies to clearly label their products.

Complete the outline notes below. You can look at the passage if you want.

TRANS FATS

1 General information
- the result of an **1.** _____ process
- also called "partially hydrogenated oils"
- occur in small amounts in many kinds of **2.** _____

2 Until 1960s
- 1890s   the process of hydrogenated oils
    - → **3.** _____ by Paul Sabatier
    - → the production of **4.** _____
- 1920   <u>Crisco</u> first went on sale
    - = a **5.** _____ replacement in baking bread, pie, cookies, and cakes

3 Scientific studies
- 1960 onward,   trans fats = **6.** _____ for our health
- **7.** _____ → spotlight on their <u>health risks</u>
    - = heart disease, stroke, and **8.** _____
    - ← trans fats increase bad **9.** _____ levels

4 Recommendation
- keep an eye out for trans fats in your favorite foods
- limit trans-fat intake to **10.** _____ of daily calories

UNIT 1
UNIT 2
UNIT 3
UNIT 4
UNIT 5
UNIT 6
UNIT 7
UNIT 8
UNIT 9
TRANS FATS
UNIT 10
UNIT 11
UNIT 12
UNIT 13
UNIT 14

WRITING AND DISCUSSION

Read the questions below and write down your answer below. Exchange your ideas or opinions with your classmates. Use the hints if you want.

1. How do you decide what food to buy?

Hints ➡ read nutrition facts label / depend on recipe /

buy what I want to eat

Your Ideas

....
....
....
....
....

2. How will your eating habits change if you try to avoid trans fats?

Hints ➡ cook by myself / snacks / instant foods

Your Ideas

....
....
....
....
....

FURTHER STUDY
ActeaBo

For further study, access ActeaBo and review today's lesson.

http://acteabo.jp

Braille

WARM-UP QUESTIONS

Discuss the questions below with your classmates.

1. How would you communicate with someone you could not see?

2. Do you know any military communication systems? What are they?

VOCABULARY CD 20

From the choices below, choose the word which fits best in each sentence.

1. We have five senses — touch, _____, hearing, smell, and taste.

2. From the sky, cars look like little _____ on the landscape.

3. In front of the palace, I saw a few _____ guarding the main gate.

4. Should the union accept or _____ the party's leading role?

5. A pool lifeguard tried to revive her and called an ambulance _____.

6. She arranges thin _____, squares, and triangles in complex patterns.

7. The staff has been placing these labels _____ on the case.

8. That beautiful chapel could only _____ a fraction of the people.

9. We all know the chemical _____ for helium is He.

10. The boy apologized _____ times to his teacher for his attitude.

accommodate	countless	dots	horizontally	immediately
rectangles	reject	sight	soldiers	symbol

Time order (2)

In addition to the time words introduced in Unit 9, the words below are also useful for understanding time order.

Example

Verb	begin, end
Adverb	later, nowadays
Conjunction	after, before, since, when

EXERCISE

Focus on time words and expressions in Paragraphs 1 to 3 of the passage on p. 66. Compare your notes with your classmates.

Time words	Notes

⌄ The statue of Louis Braille at his
birthplace (cc by Kou07kou)

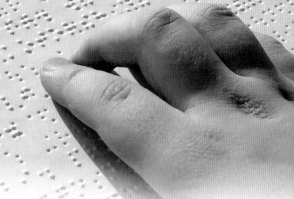

READING PASSAGE 🎵 21

Read the passage below and pay attention to time order.

1   Just because people lose their sight does not mean that they cannot read anymore. They just learn to read in a different way.

2   Blind people read by running their fingers over pages that have groups of tiny raised dots. These dots represent different letters, and they form an
5 alphabet that is just like ours. This writing system is called braille.

3   Braille has a very interesting history. Its story begins around 1800, when a French soldier named Charles Barbier created a system of raised dots so that soldiers could read messages in the dark. Napoléon wanted his troops to be able to communicate in the dark without giving away their positions. In the
10 end, this so-called "night writing" system was too complicated for soldiers to learn. It had to be rejected by the military.

4   Years later, Charles Barbier met Louis Braille at the National Institute for the Blind in Paris. Louis Braille had been blind since the age of four, and he immediately recognized both the potential importance of Barbier's system and
15 its major flaw. Louis set to work on making it easier to use, and eventually the braille system was born.

≫ Braille alphabet cells

5   In braille, each letter, or cell, is made up of a rectangle in which there can be a combination of up to six raised

20 dots or an absence of dots. The six dots are arranged in a grid of two dots horizontally by three dots vertically. The dots are numbered 1, 2, and 3 from top to bottom on the left column and 4, 5, and 6

⌃ Perkins NEXTGEN Brailler

25 from top to bottom on the right column. There can be 64 different combinations. Braille has also evolved to accommodate differences in other languages. For example, Greek braille is different from Chinese braille.

6   Blind people can also write in braille. Most use a special typewriter, called the Perkins Brailler, which types braille onto paper. Nowadays, computer

30 keyboards with braille symbols are also available.

7   It is amazing that a military technology from the Napoleonic Wars has grown into something that has improved the lives of countless blind people around the world.

▌ COMPREHENSION QUESTIONS

Decide if each statement is true [T] or false [F]. If it is false, write the sentence correctly.

1. [   ] Napoleon wanted his troops to have a way to communicate in the dark.

2. [   ] Louis Braille, whom Charles met in Paris, had been blind since his childhood.

3. [   ] Six dots are arranged in a grid of two dots vertically by three dots horizontally.

4. [   ] There are dots numbered 1, 2, and 3 from top to bottom on the left column.

5. [   ] Greek braille is different from that of other countries like Japan.

GRAPHIC SUMMARY

Complete the outline notes below. You can look at the passage if you want.

BRAILLE

1 Blind people
- no sense of 1.   → learn to read in a different way

    = run their 2.   over pages to read

       tiny raised 3.

          = different letters
          = braille

2 Its history
- around 1800   Charles Barbier (a French Soldier)

              "night writing" system

                   = soldiers read messages in the 4.

                   too 5.   to learn

              rejected by the military

- years later   Louis Braille

              recognized potential and major 6.   of

              "night writing" system

                   making it easier

              braille system

3 Its system
- made up of a 7.
- → a combination of up to 8.   raised dots or absence of dots
- 64 different 9.   → in other languages
- a special typewriter = the Perkins Brailler
- nowadays = computer keyboards → improve the lives of

    10.   blind people

WRITING AND DISCUSSION

Read the questions below and write down your answer below.
Exchange your ideas or opinions with your classmates. Use the hints
if you want.

1. Do you think we need to make a new common language? Why?

> *Hints* ➡ communicate easily / understand culture /
> need time and efforts

> **Your Ideas**
> ....
> ....
> ....
> ....
> ....

2. How can we communicate with people who do not share a common language with us?

> *Hints* ➡ draw pictures / study their languages / use gestures

> **Your Ideas**
> ....
> ....
> ....
> ....
> ....

FURTHER STUDY

For further study, access ActeaBo and review today's lesson.

http://acteabo.jp

UNIT **11**

Cause and Effect

Nightmares

WARM-UP QUESTIONS

Discuss the questions below with your classmates.

1. What kind of dreams do you often have?

2. Do you tell other people about them? Why or why not?

VOCABULARY   🎧 22

From the choices below, choose the word which fits best in each sentence.

1. It is natural for you to feel a genuine sense of _____ of death.

2. I had another terrible nightmare and could not shake the _____ images from my mind.

3. They are going to examine the _____ composition of the liquids.

4. A convicted killer who _____ from an Iowa prison is on the loose.

5. All the buildings in my town are _____ by underground passages.

6. The government deployed additional military forces to _____ terrorists.

7. This method can change the activity of certain nerve cells and influence the _____.

8. Everyone gets feelings of sadness or _____, but most of them are short-lived.

9. These editing _____ have been used on many photos posted on social media.

10. She spent a lot of time practicing for the competition and _____ her performance.

attack	brain	chemical	connected	depression
escaped	fear	rehearsing	techniques	vivid

Cause and Effect (1)

Some passages explain causes and effects. In this case, focusing on the words or expressions below can help you understand the passage structure more easily.

Example

Cause	cause, one reason is ~, because
Effect	result in, lead to, influence, so, as a result

EXERCISE

Read the Paragraph 2 of the passage on p. 72, focusing on words or expressions of cause and effect, and take notes. Compare your notes with your classmates.

Cause and effect expressions	Notes

Read the passage below and pay attention to its structure.

1 Many of us have woken up in the night, covered in cold sweat and feeling a deep sense of fear. Terrible images flash through your head as you recall the horrifying things you have just experienced. This is often followed a few moments later by a sigh of relief, though. It was all just a bad dream.

5 **2** Nightmares are vivid dreams that tear you out of a deep sleep and leave you with a strong negative emotion. In the past, people thought that nightmares were caused by an evil spirit called a mare, which tormented sleepers with bad dreams—hence the name "nightmare." Now, however, we know that nightmares can be caused by both psychological and chemical 10 factors.

3 Stress and worry are two of the most common causes of nightmares. Adults may have dreams in which they are unable to escape from danger or are falling from a great height. These kinds of nightmares are usually connected to strong doubts or fears they have at work or in their personal 15 lives. Repeated nightmares can also come after experiencing something

≫ Getting professional help can help you get rid of bad dreams.

⌃ Nightmares are vivid dreams that leave you with a strong negative emotion.

>> Repeated nightmares can come after scary experiences.

particularly scary or upsetting, such as being attacked or witnessing a violent event. People will often relive these events night after night during their sleep, and it can sometimes take professional
20 help to rid them of these bad dreams.

4   Another reason for nightmares, and one that is easier to avoid, is eating late-night snacks. Eating food late at night means your brain will be more active when you sleep, and so you are more likely to have vivid, realistic, and often frightening dreams. Additionally, taking certain types of drugs, especially
25 ones that affect chemicals in the brain such as those that combat depression, is likely to lead to nightmares.

5   If your sleep is often disturbed by the same nightmare, there is a simple technique that you can perform to stop it. You should try to think up an alternate, happy ending to your nightmare and rehearse it in your mind while
30 you are awake. Think about it again just before you go to sleep, and your mind should replace the frightening ending with the happy one you have rehearsed. Sweet dreams!

COMPREHENSION QUESTIONS
Decide if each statement is true [T] or false [F]. If it is false, write the sentence correctly.

1. [   ] People's minds sometimes flash back to horrifying things they have experienced.

2. [   ] People in the past believed in an evil spirit called a mare, which make sleepers suffer a lot.

3. [   ] Professional help can sometimes get rid of repeated nightmares.

4. [   ] You are likely to have vivid, realistic, and often frightening dreams if you eat late at night.

5. [   ] Your mind should replace the frightening ending with the happy one you have experienced.

Complete the outline notes below. You can look at the passage if you want.

NIGHTMARES

1 What are they?

- = vivid dreams
  - tear you out of a **1.** _____ sleep
  - leave you with a strong negative **2.** _____
- past : by an **3.** _____ spirit

  now : by psychological and chemical factors

2 Their causes

- stress and worry: **4.** _____ causes

  e.g.) adult's dream: cannot escape from danger or falling from a

  great height

  ← strong **5.** _____ or fears
- very scary or upsetting **6.** _____ : **7.** _____

  nightmares
- eating **8.** _____ snacks: brain will be active when you

  sleep
- some drugs: affect **9.** _____ in your brain
  - e.g.) depression

3 Simple technique

- try to think up a happy **10.** _____ to the nightmare
- rehearse it in your mind when you are awake
- think about it again before sleep

UNIT 1
UNIT 2
UNIT 3
UNIT 4
UNIT 5
UNIT 6
UNIT 7
UNIT 8
UNIT 9
UNIT 10
UNIT 11
UNIT 12
UNIT 13
UNIT 14

NIGHTMARES

WRITING AND DISCUSSION

Read the questions below and write down your answer below.
Exchange your ideas or opinions with your classmates. Use the hints
if you want.

1. What do you usually do to relieve stress?

Hints ➲ watch movies / talk with my friends or family /
just sleep

> Your Ideas
>
> ....
> ....
> ....
> ....
> ....

2. What do you think makes you sleep well?

Hints ➲ listen to music / use a comfortable pillow / exercise

> Your Ideas
>
> ....
> ....
> ....
> ....
> ....

FURTHER STUDY
ActeaBo

For further study, access ActeaBo and review today's lesson.

http://acteabo.jp

75

Cause and Effect

The Power of Positive Thinking

WARM-UP QUESTIONS

Discuss the questions below with your classmates.

1. In what kind of situations do you feel bad?
2. Do you think you are a positive or negative thinker? Why?

VOCABULARY   24

From the choices below, choose the word which fits best in each sentence.

1. My son _____ his experiences in a letter to his grandparents.
2. The leader is responsible for the success or _____ of his plans.
3. She suddenly _____ her boyfriend to her previous one when we were talking.
4. I decided to do something more productive than to _____ on the past.
5. How do you _____ spend the 40-minute lunch break in your university?
6. Developmental _____ is the study of how and why human beings change over time.
7. We now have a week to rest, recover, and _____ from our injuries.
8. Some of the girls tried to _____ his attention but failed.
9. A few of the _____ who were held by the terrorists were reported to be alive.
10. Our life has drastically _____ since we changed our eating habits.

attract	compared	described	dwell	failure
generally	heal	hostages	improved	psychology

Cause and Effect (2)

In addition to those introduced in Unit 11, below are some other examples of words or expressions of cause and effect.

Example

Cause	affect, due to, result from
Effect	improve, benefit, consequently

EXERCISE

Read Paragraph 2 of the passage on p. 78, focusing on words or expressions of cause and effect, and take notes. Compare your notes with your classmates.

Cause and effect expressions	Notes

Read the passage below and pay attention to its structure.

1   There is a glass on the table, filled up halfway with water. How would you describe the glass: half empty or half full? If your answer was "half full," then prepare yourself for an exciting life in which anything is possible. If you said "half empty" on the other hand, you might just be in for a life of failure
5 and sorrow. It may sound crazy, but that is the mysterious power of positive thinking!

2   Experts believe that positive thinking has several important benefits. First off, it can make us feel happy about our life. If someone focuses on all of the good things that they have, he is much less likely to feel bad about his
10 life. Compare that to someone who is always complaining and dwelling on the negative side of any situation. The positive thinker will generally be the happier of the two.

3   Positive thinking can also improve our health. Several studies have shown that human biology is linked with psychology. One study in particular revealed
15 that wounds take longer to heal for people who are exposed to depressing situations in their job. It has also been proven that people who are highly stressed are more susceptible to catching a cold and the flu.

4 Some people even believe that positive thinking can affect the

20 world around us. In the 2006 book *The Secret*, author Rhonda Byrne describes a "law of attraction." This law is based on the notion that positive thinking attracts positive

25 things, and negative thinking attracts negative things. Thus, if you think about a new sports car, you might just get one. But whatever you do, try not to think about being taken hostage at the bank!

⌃ If someone practices smiling every day, he or she will think happier thoughts.

30 **5** Positive thinking may improve our minds, bodies, and even the universe around us, but how do we get started? According to Richard Wiseman, a former magician turned professor of psychology, the best way to change how we think is to change our behavior. He believes that if someone practices smiling every day, he or she will think happier thoughts.

COMPREHENSION QUESTIONS

Decide if each statement is true [T] or false [F]. If it is false, write the sentence correctly.

1. [   ] If you thought a glass filled up halfway with water was half empty, you might become successful.

2. [   ] Positive thinkers are generally happier than negative thinkers.

3. [   ] It has been proven that stressed people are more likely to suffer from colds or the flu.

4. [   ] Thinking about a new sports car and being taken hostage at a bank are negative thinking.

5. [   ] Positive thinking may improve our minds and bodies, but not the universe around us.

Complete the outline notes below. You can look at the passage if you want.

THE POWER OF POSITIVE THINKING

1 Its benefits

- makes us feel ___1.___ about our life

  ↔ complaining and dwelling on the ___2.___ side

- ___3.___ our health

  ← human biology = ___4.___

  e.g.) wounds of depressed people

  → take longer to ___5.___

- ___6.___ the world around us: *The Secret* by Rhonda
  Byrne

  "law of ___7.___"

  = ___8.___ thinking = positive things

  negative thinking = negative things

2 How to change our thinking

- change our ___9.___ (by Richard Wiseman)

  e.g.) practice ___10.___ every day → happier thoughts

WRITING AND DISCUSSION

Read the questions below and write down your answer below.
Exchange your ideas or opinions with your classmates. Use the hints
if you want.

1. How do you think positively when you fail at something?

   Hints ➲ forget everything / reflect on what I did / talk with
   someone

   > Your Ideas
   >
   > ....
   >
   > ....
   >
   > ....
   >
   > ....

2. What would you do if your friends or family suffered from depression?

   Hints ➲ search for information / keep talking /
   behave the same as before

   > Your Ideas
   >
   > ....
   >
   > ....
   >
   > ....
   >
   > ....

FURTHER STUDY

For further study, access ActeaBo and review today's lesson.

http://acteabo.jp

UNIT **13**

The Andes Mountain Range

WARM-UP QUESTIONS

Discuss the questions below with your classmates.

1. Which country has well-known mountains?
2. Do you like climbing? Why or why not?

VOCABULARY 🔊 26

From the choices below, choose the word which fits best in each sentence.

1. The thought of the accident sent chills up my _____.
2. He made another attempt at climbing to the _____ of the mountain.
3. Most of us know a little over 70 percent of the Earth's _____ is covered in water.
4. The organization has worked to protect cultural and biological _____ for decades.
5. The house has been well maintained and is in excellent _____.
6. A man _____ from a dark alleyway when I was walking home last night.
7. The British Isles are famous for their _____ weather.
8. The general said that _____ the capital city was not the only way to win the war.
9. We plan to _____ the surrounding areas and take in as much of the local culture as possible.
10. With its beautiful streets and architecture, Prague is one of the most _____ cities in Europe.

condition	conquering	diversity	emerged	explore
majestic	peak	spine	surface	unpredictable

Guessing the meaning of unfamiliar words (1)

When reading, you may come across unfamiliar words. It is important to use a dictionary to look up the meaning. However, it is also important to try to guess the meaning beforehand and engage your brain. Follow these suggestions to guess the meanings of words you do not know.

1. Check the words before and after unfamiliar words and use them as hints.
2. Try to guess the meaning of the unfamiliar word.
3. If you cannot guess, look for hints from other parts of the text.
4. Use a dictionary to check the meaning.

▌ *EXERCISE*

Try to guess the meaning of the first two words you do not know in the passage on p. 84. Use a dictionary to check the meaning.

Unfamiliar words	Meanings
1.	
2.	

READING PASSAGE   27

*Read the passage below and guess the
meanings of unfamiliar words.*

1   Look at a map of South America, and you
will see a long, curving spine of mountains
running down the entire western coast of the
continent. This enormous stretch of volcanic
5 peaks and lofty ridges runs from north to south
through a total of seven countries and covers a distance of over 7,000 km,
passing through the equator and ending near the icy waters of the Antarctic
Ocean.

2   The Andes have an average height of 4,000 meters above sea level, and
10 their highest peak, Aconcagua, reaches an altitude of 6,962 m. This makes the
Andes the highest mountain range outside Asia. The Himalayas are, of course,
the highest mountain range in the world; however, due to the fact that the
Andes pass through the equator, the summit of Mount Chimborazo in Ecuador
is the point on the earth's surface that is farthest from the earth's core.

15 **3**   The Andes are an area of stunning diversity in landscape, climate,
wildlife, and plants. The northern part of the Andes is humid, hot, and rainy—
conditions perfect for rainforests. Indeed, the Amazon rain forest borders
much of the northern Andes, and the mighty Amazon River even begins its life
as a small trickle of water emerging from a cliff face high up in the mountains.
20 The central region is milder, while the southern Andes are cold and largely

Aconcagua in Argentina is the
highest peak in the Andes.
(cc by Daniel Peppes Gauer)

uninhabited. The climate in the Andes can be so unpredictable that the local residents say they often experience "four seasons in one day."

4   Despite its changeable climate, one of the most important civilizations of the last thousand years—the Incan civilization—developed in the Andes.
25 The Incans carved terraces into the steep slopes of the mountains to grow crops such as potatoes and corn. In 1532, the Spanish conquered the Incans. The name Andes is thought by some to come from the Spanish word "andén," which means "platform."

5   The Spanish built a colonial city in Quito, which now attracts thousands
30 of tourists every year. From the city, tourists can take day trips to go hiking, climbing, river rafting, and exploring, all while enjoying the majestic beauty of the Andes.

Quito is packed with historical monuments and architectural treasures.

Historic colonial buildings in Quito

COMPREHENSION QUESTIONS

Decide if each statement is true [T] or false [F]. If it is false, write the sentence correctly.

1. [   ] The Andes are a long spine of mountains running from west to east in South America.

2. [   ] Aconcagua is the highest peak in the Himalayas, a mountain range outside Asia.

3. [   ] The world's highest summit is not the farthest one from the earth's core.

4. [   ] A cliff face in the northern Andes is the birthplace of the Amazon River.

5. [   ] The Incans built terraced fields to grow crops such as potatoes and corns.

≪ An ancient Incan city in the Andes

GRAPHIC SUMMARY

Complete the outline notes below. You can look at the passage if you want.

THE ANDES MOUNTAIN RANGE

1 Location
- in South America
- **1.** _____ from north to south through 7 countries
- 7,000 km long

2 The highest mountain?
- **2.** _____ : 4,0000 m on average
  : 6,962 m on the highest (= Aconcagua)
  = highest outside Asia,
    but farthest from the earth's core
    ← pass through the **3.** _____

3 Climate
- diverse **4.** _____
  - northern part : **5.** _____, hot, rainy
    e.g.) Amazon rainforest
  - central part : milder
  - southern part : cold, uninhabited
- **6.** _____ climate = "four seasons in one day"

4 Civilization
- **7.** _____ : carved terraces to grow **8.** _____
    cf. **2.** _____ = "platform" in
      Spanish
- **9.** _____ by the Spanish in 1532
  cf. Quito:once colonial city
    :now **10.** _____ many tourists

WRITING AND DISCUSSION

Read the questions below and write down your answer below. Exchange your ideas or opinions with your classmates. Use the hints if you want.

1. What do you think are the benefits of climbing mountains?

   Hints ➲ heal / memory / accomplishment

   Your Ideas

   ....

   ....

   ....

   ....

2. How do you try to get rid of your stress?

   Hints ➲ play sports / watch TV / talk with friends

   Your Ideas

   ....

   ....

   ....

   ....

FURTHER STUDY

For further study, access ActeaBo and review today's lesson.

http://acteabo.jp

UNIT 1
UNIT 2
UNIT 3
UNIT 4
UNIT 5
UNIT 6
UNIT 7
UNIT 8
UNIT 9
UNIT 10
UNIT 11
UNIT 12
UNIT 13
UNIT 14

THE ANDES MOUNTAIN RANGE

UNIT **14**

Freedom Riders

WARM-UP QUESTIONS

Discuss the questions below with your classmates.

1. In our society, what kind of system or situation do you want to change? Why?

2. What actions are you taking to change it?

VOCABULARY   🔊 28

From the choices below, choose the word which fits best in each sentence.

1. The students led a _____ to protest the destruction of the rain forest.

2. They wanted a society based on _____ for all people, regardless of gender, race, or religion.

3. The first chapter of the book contained general _____ information on the history of the Internet.

4. This cosmopolitan city attracts people from a broad range of _____ and ethnic groups.

5. My sister wants to live in a house that has a bathroom and a _____ toilet.

6. The newspaper published a photo of rioters being _____ by the police.

7. Our university has a world-famous research _____.

8. Most elderly people tend to _____ the idea of living in a nursing home.

9. The expert says _____ are weapons that should be used against enemies in war.

10. Last year it was reported that the suspected terrorist was _____ in North Africa.

arrested	background	beaten	equality	facility
firebombs	movement	racial	resist	separate

Guessing the meaning of unfamiliar words (2)

For guessing the meaning of the unfamiliar word, grammatical structure can also give you a good hint.

Example   She had her own door keys <u>dangling</u> on a chain.

   no be-verb before

   → explains "keys"

EXERCISE

Try to guess the meaning of the first two words you do not know in the passage on p. 90. Use a dictionary to check the meaning.

Unknown words	Meanings
1.	
2.	

READING PASSAGE   29

Read the passage below and guess the meanings of unfamiliar words.

1 The African-American Civil Rights movement was a struggle from 1955 to 1968 to achieve equal rights for black people in the United States. It involved the hard work of
5 thousands of people all over the country, and all with one goal in mind: equality for everyone.

2 The Freedom Riders were one segment of this massive movement. They were people of all ages and different backgrounds who wanted to challenge the racial segregation
10 laws that existed in the southern United States. At the time, all buses, trains, and airplanes in the south had separate facilities for white and black people. However, the US Supreme Court had ruled that it was illegal to have segregated seating on any bus that crossed state lines. So the Freedom
15 Riders would fill a bus with mixed races in a northern state and get off in the south, in defiance of the local laws.

3 This might sound like a minor protest now, but it was a huge deal at the time. When the original 13 Freedom Riders went on their first bus ride into the south, they were beaten
20 several times. No matter how bad it got, they never fought back. They firmly believed in the concept of nonviolent resistance.

⌃ **Martin Luther King, Jr. at a Civil Rights March on Washington, DC (1963)**

⌃ Robert F. Kennedy speaking to a Civil Rights crowd in 1963

⌄ Civil Rights march in Washington (1963)

≫ Freedom Rider Jim Zwerg in 1961 after being beaten

90

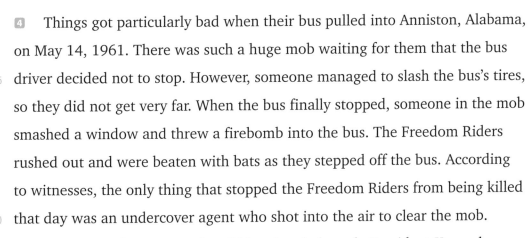

4   Things got particularly bad when their bus pulled into Anniston, Alabama,
on May 14, 1961. There was such a huge mob waiting for them that the bus

25 driver decided not to stop. However, someone managed to slash the bus's tires,
so they did not get very far. When the bus finally stopped, someone in the mob
smashed a window and threw a firebomb into the bus. The Freedom Riders
rushed out and were beaten with bats as they stepped off the bus. According
to witnesses, the only thing that stopped the Freedom Riders from being killed

30 that day was an undercover agent who shot into the air to clear the mob.

5   As more and more Freedom Riders headed south, President Kennedy
became alarmed at the violence. He struck a deal with southern governments
that they could arrest the Freedom Riders as long as they kept them safe. Still,
the Riders kept coming, until eventually the segregation laws were changed.

« Some freedom riders were
jailed in the Mississippi State
Penitentiary.

COMPREHENSION QUESTIONS

*Decide if each statement is true [T] or false [F]. If it is false, write
the sentence correctly.*

1. [   ] Movements to help black people involved the hard work of
          thousands of individuals in the United States.

2. [   ] Black people were challenging the racial segregation laws
          everywhere in the U.S.

3. [   ] The Freedom Riders filled a bus with mixed races in a northern
          state and got off in the south.

4. [   ] Although the bus tires were slashed by someone in the mob,
          the bus was not seriously damaged.

5. [   ] President Kennedy made southern states promise not to arrest
          the Freedom Riders.

Complete the outline notes below. You can look at the passage if you want.

FREEDOM RIDERS

1 **Civil Rights movements**

- from 1955 to 1968 in the US

  the **1.** _____ Civil Rights movement

  → to achieve equal rights for **2.** _____ people

  → one goal = **3.** _____ for everyone

- the Freedom Riders = all ages and different **4.** _____

  = challenge the racial **5.** _____ laws

  e.g.) bus, train, and airplanes with **6.** _____

  seating for white and black people

- the original **7.** _____ Freedom Riders:

  bus ride into the south → beaten

  BUT

  never fought back ← the concept of **8.** _____

  resistance

2 **A huge deal**

- May 14, 1961 in Alabama: a huge **9.** _____

  - smashed a window

  - threw a firebomb into the bus

  ↓

  more and more Freedom Riders

- President Kennedy: was **10.** _____ at the violence

  ↓

- still, the Riders kept coming

  ↓

- the segregation laws were changed

WRITING AND DISCUSSION

Read the questions below and write down your answer below.
Exchange your ideas or opinions with your classmates. Use the hints if you want.

1. How do you protest against people or organizations which do not accept your ideas?

Hints ➲ cooperate with others / do nothing / boycott

> **Your Ideas**
>
> ....
> ....
> ....
> ....
> ....

2. How do you deal with protests from others?

Hints ➲ ask experts for help / discuss my views with them / reflect by yourself

> **Your Ideas**
>
> ....
> ....
> ....
> ....
> ....

FURTHER STUDY

For further study, access ActeaBo and review today's lesson.

http://acteabo.jp

FREEDOM RIDERS

Tips for Reading: Reflecting on your study

Now that you have completed this textbook, how much have your English abilities improved? On Page 7, you set your goal and smaller steps. How many steps have you taken now?

Now is the time for you to stop and reflect on your learning.

- How much have you achieved?
- Was your method of learning OK?
- Is there anything you should change? If so, how?

LET'S TRY

Reflect on your English learning.

Your original goal	
Your original smaller steps	
How much you have achieved	
Things to change	

TEXT PRODUCTION STAFF

edited by	編集
Takashi Kudo	工藤 隆志

cover design by	表紙デザイン
Nobuyoshi Fujino	藤野 伸芳

text design by	本文デザイン
Nobuyoshi Fujino	藤野 伸芳

CD PRODUCTION STAFF

recorded by	吹き込み者
Neil DeMaere (AmE)	ニール・デマル（アメリカ英語）

Success with Reading Book 2 —Boost Your Reading Skills—
リーディング力アップのための7つの方略 Book 2

2020年1月20日　初版発行
2024年1月30日　第6刷発行

著　者	池田　真生子
	清水　綾香
	Zachary Fillingham
	Owain Mckimm
	Judy Majewski
発 行 者	佐野 英一郎
発 行 所	株式会社 成美堂
	〒101-0052　東京都千代田区神田小川町3-22
	TEL 03-3291-2261　FAX 03-3293-5490
	https://www.seibido.co.jp

印刷・製本　(株)加藤文明社

ISBN 978-4-7919-7202-9　　　　　　　　　　　　　　　Printed in Japan